I am CARED For

30 TRUTHS FROM GOD TO KEEP CAREGIVERS ENCOURAGED

Published by The Tree of Love, LLC
https://thetreeoflove.org/

Printed in the United States of America

Scripture Pages, Prayer, Truths of God, & Back Matter by Michelle Post, Ph.D.

Book Cover & Coloring Pages by Digitalworld25

This Coloring Book Belongs To:

_____

I am Cared For

Cast all your anxiety on him because he cares for you.
1 Peter 5:7 NIV

Prayer of God's Care For You

Heavenly Father, thank You for the person reading this prayer. I ask in Jesus name that You will show them how much You care for them. Hold them tight, give them strength, comfort them, and renew their Spirit daily. Amen.

The Truths of Who God Is
. . . Just a Few

- **God is Love** - The one who does not love does not know God, for God is love. 1 John 4:8 NASB
- **God is Truth** - For His lovingkindness is great toward us, and the truth of the Lord is everlasting. Praise the Lord! Psalm 117:2 NASB
- **God is Good** - For You, Lord, are good, and ready to forgive, and abundant in lovingkindness to all who call upon You. Psalm 86:5 NASB
- **God is Trustworthy** - . . . so that by two unchangeable things in which it is impossible for God to lie, we who have taken refuge would have strong encouragement to take hold of the hope set before us. Hebrews 6:18 NASB
- **God is Forgiving** - For you, O Lord, are good and forgiving, abounding in steadfast love to all who call upon you. Psalm 86:5 ESV
- **God is Just** - The Rock, his work is perfect, for all his ways are justice. A God of faithfulness and without iniquity, just and upright is He. Deuteronomy 32:4 ESV
- **God is Everywhere** - In the beginning was the Word, and the Word was with God, and the Word was God. He was in the beginning with God. All things were made through him, and without him was not any thing made that was made. In him was life,[a] and the life was the light of men. The light shines in the darkness, and the darkness has not overcome it. John 1:1-5 ESV
- **God is Faithful** - Know therefore that the LORD your God is God; he is the faithful God, keeping his covenant of love to a thousand generations of those who love him and keep his commandments. Deuteronomy 7:9 NIV
- **God is Gracious** - Gracious is the Lord, and righteous; yes, our God is compassionate. Psalm 116:5 NASB
- **God is Merciful** - Then the Lord passed by in front of him and proclaimed, "The Lord, the Lord God, compassionate and gracious, slow to anger, and abounding in lovingkindness and truth . . . Exodus 34:6 NASB
- **God is Constant** - Every good thing given and every perfect gift is from above, coming down from the Father of lights, with whom there is no variation or shifting shadow. James 1:17 NASB
- **God is All-Knowing** - For the word of God is living and active, sharper than any two-edged sword, piercing to the division of soul and of spirit, of joints and of marrow, and discerning the thoughts and intentions of the heart. And no creature is hidden from his sight, but all are naked and exposed to the eyes of him to whom we must give account. Hebrews 4:12-13 ESV

I am
Finding
Rest

MATTHEW 11:28 NASB

I am Finding Rest

Come to Me, all who are weary and burdened, and I will give you rest.
Matthew 11:28 NASB

I AM IN

PERFECT

PEACE

ISAIAH 26:3-4 NIV

I am in Perfect Peace

You will keep in perfect peace those whose minds are steadfast, because they trust in you. Trust in the Lord forever, for the Lord, the Lord himself, is the Rock eternal.
Isaiah 26:3-4 NIV

I am Held

ISAIAH 41:10 NKJV

I am Held

Fear not, for I am with you; be not dismayed, for I am your God. I will strengthen you, yes, I will help you, I will uphold you with My righteous right hand.
Isaiah 41:10 NKJV

I am

Not

Stressing

PSALM 119:143 NLT

I am Not Stressing

As pressure and stress bear down on me, I find joy in your commands.
Psalm 119:143 NLT

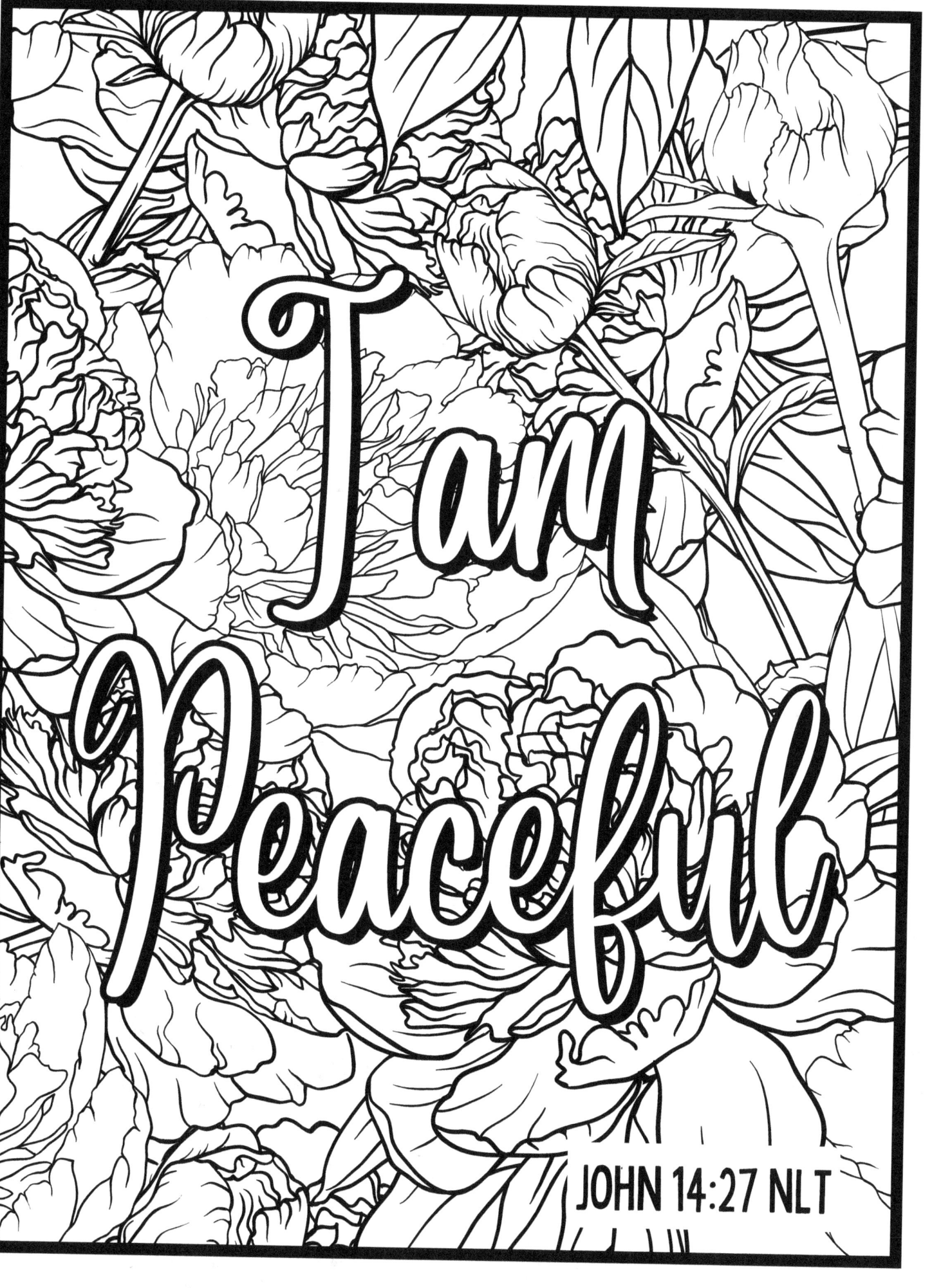

I am Peaceful

JOHN 14:27 NLT

I am Peaceful

I am leaving you with a gift—peace of mind and heart. And the peace I give is a gift the world cannot give. So don't be troubled or afraid.

John 14:27 NLT

I am Helped

ISAIAH 41:13 NKJV

I am Helped

For I, the Lord your God, will hold your right hand, Saying to you, 'Fear not, I will help you.'
Isaiah 41:13 NKJV

I am Quieted by His Love

ZEPHANIAH 3:17 NKJV

I am Quieted by His Love

The Lord your God in your midst, The Mighty One, will save; He will rejoice over you with gladness, He will quiet you with His love, He will rejoice over you with singing.
Zephaniah 3:17 NKJV

I am Safe

PSALM 4:8 NLT

I am Safe

In peace I will lie down and sleep,
for you alone, O Lord, will
keep me safe.
Psalm 4:8 NLT

I am Not Troubled

JOHN 14:1 NKJV

I am Not Troubled

Let not your heart be troubled; you believe in God, believe also in Me.
John 14:1 NKJV

I am Loved Unconditionally

LAMENTATIONS 3:22-24 NIV

I am Loved Unconditionally

Because of the Lord's great love we are not consumed, for his compassions never fail. They are new every morning; great is your faithfulness. I say to myself, "The Lord is my portion; therefore I will wait for him."
Lamentations 3:22-24 NIV

I AM RESTING IN THE SHADOWS OF THE ALMIGHTY

PSALM 91:1 NIV

I am Resting in the Shadows of the Almighty

Whoever dwells in the shelter of the Most High will rest in the shadow of the Almighty.
Psalm 91:1 NIV

I am Not Worried

MATTHEW 6:25 NKJV

I am Not Worried

Therefore I say to you, do not worry about your life, what you will eat or what you will drink; nor about your body, what you will put on. Is not life more than food and the body more than clothing?
Matthew 6:25 NKJV

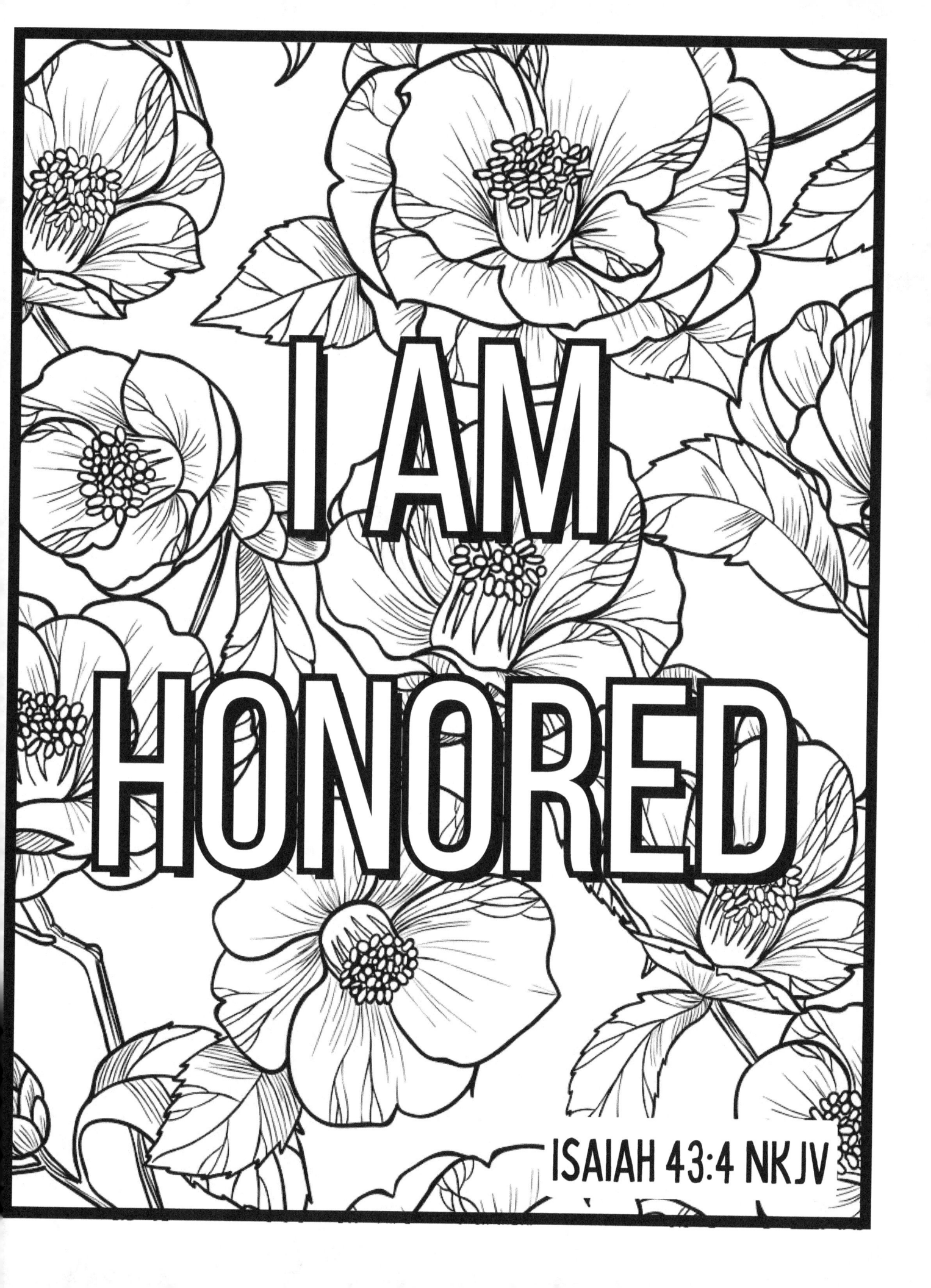

I AM

HONORED

ISAIAH 43:4 NKJV

I am Honored

Since you were precious in My sight, You have been honored, and I have loved you; therefore I will give men for you, and people for your life.
Isaiah 43:4 NKJV

I AM SUPPORTED

PSALM 94:18 NLT

I am Supported

I cried out, "I am slipping!" but
your unfailing love, O Lord,
supported me.
Psalm 94:18 NLT

I am

Established

ROMANS 8:29 NLT

I am Established

For God knew his people in advance, and he chose them to become like his Son, so that his Son would be the firstborn among many brothers and sisters.
Romans 8:29 NLT

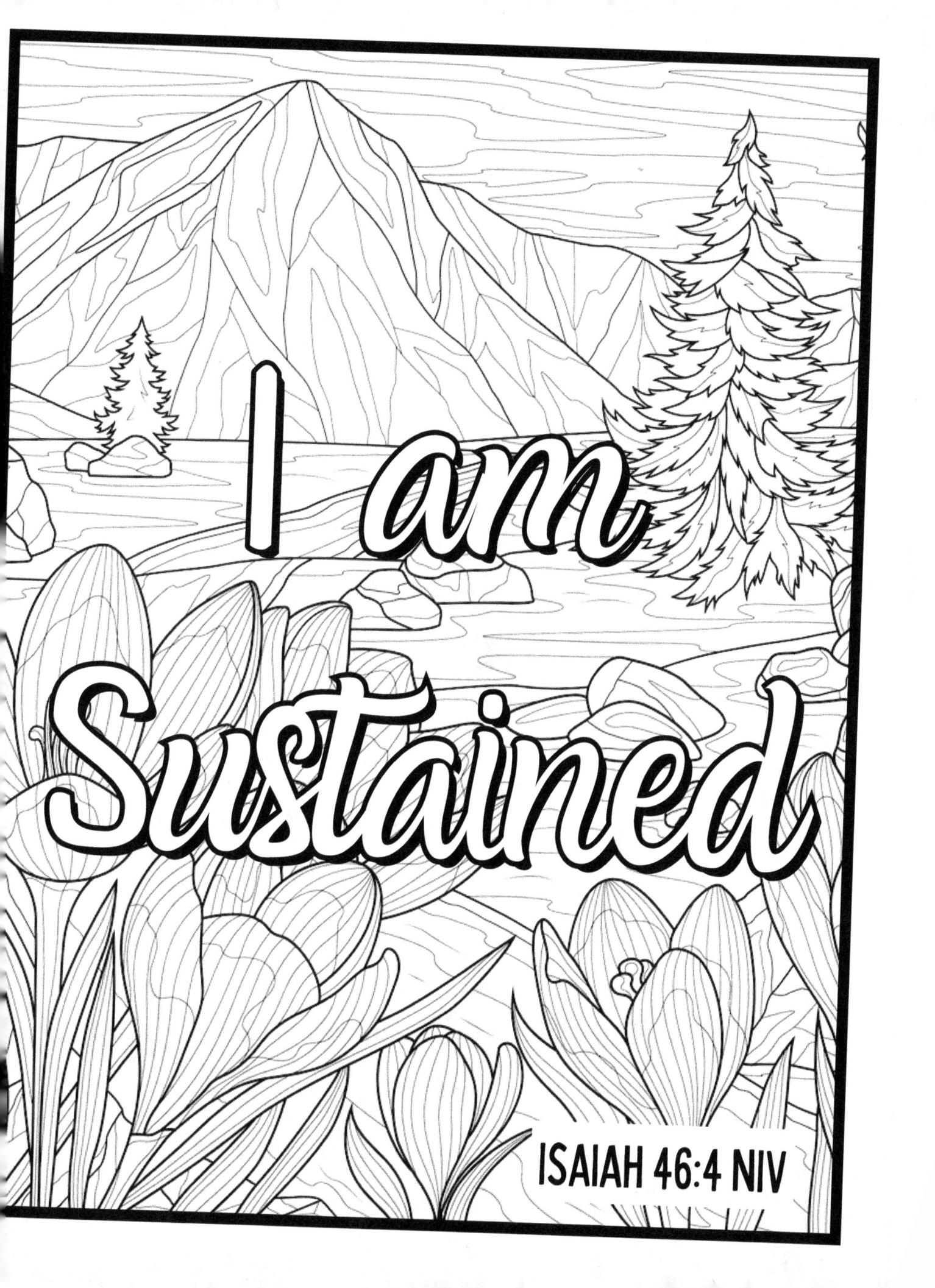

I am
Sustained

ISAIAH 46:4 NIV

I am Sustained

Even to your old age and gray hairs I am he, I am he who will sustain you. I have made you and I will carry you; I will sustain you and I will rescue you.

Isaiah 46:4 NIV

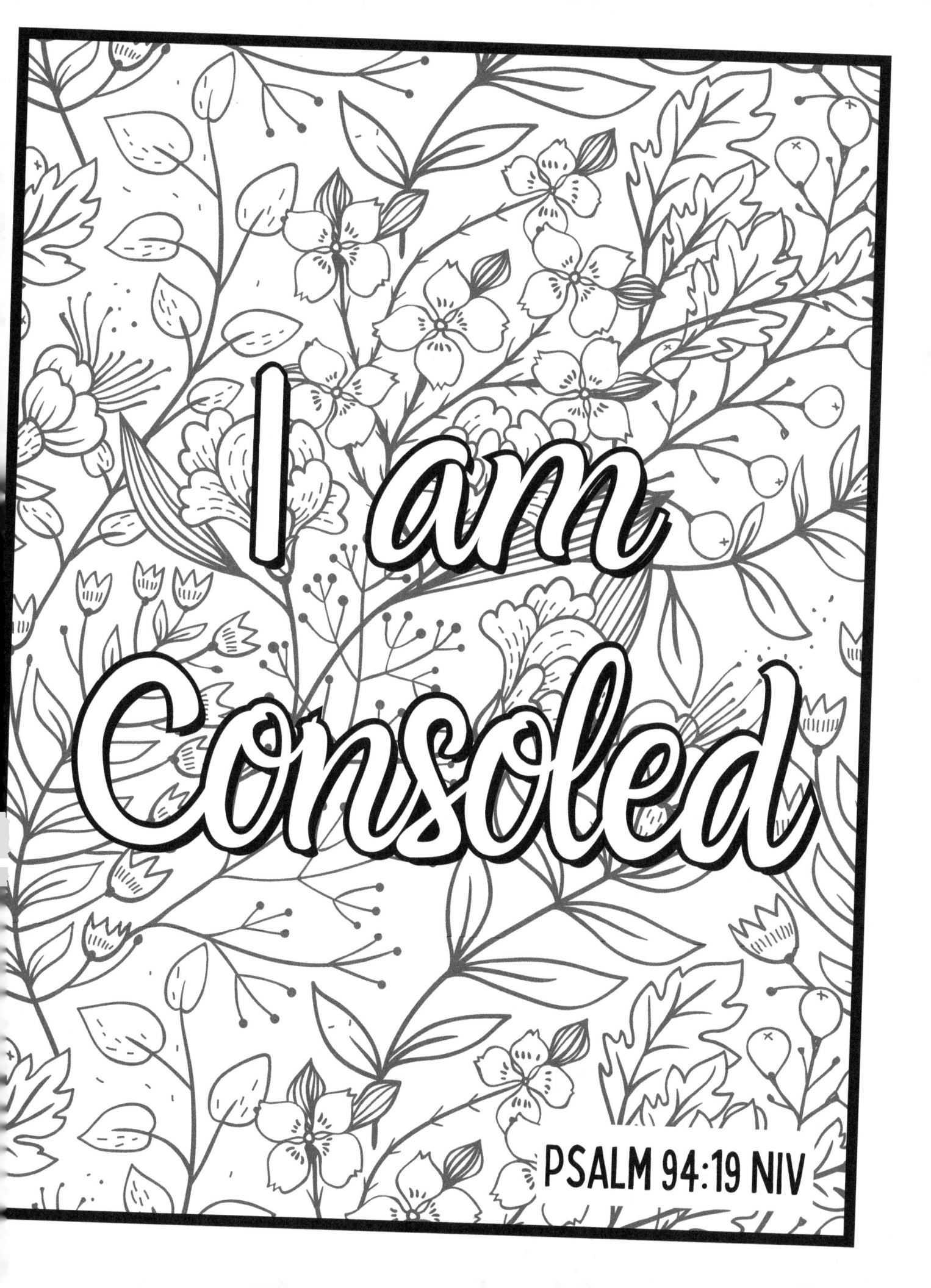

I am Consoled

PSALM 94:19 NIV

I am Consoled

When anxiety was great within me,
your consolation brought me joy.
Psalm 94:19 NIV

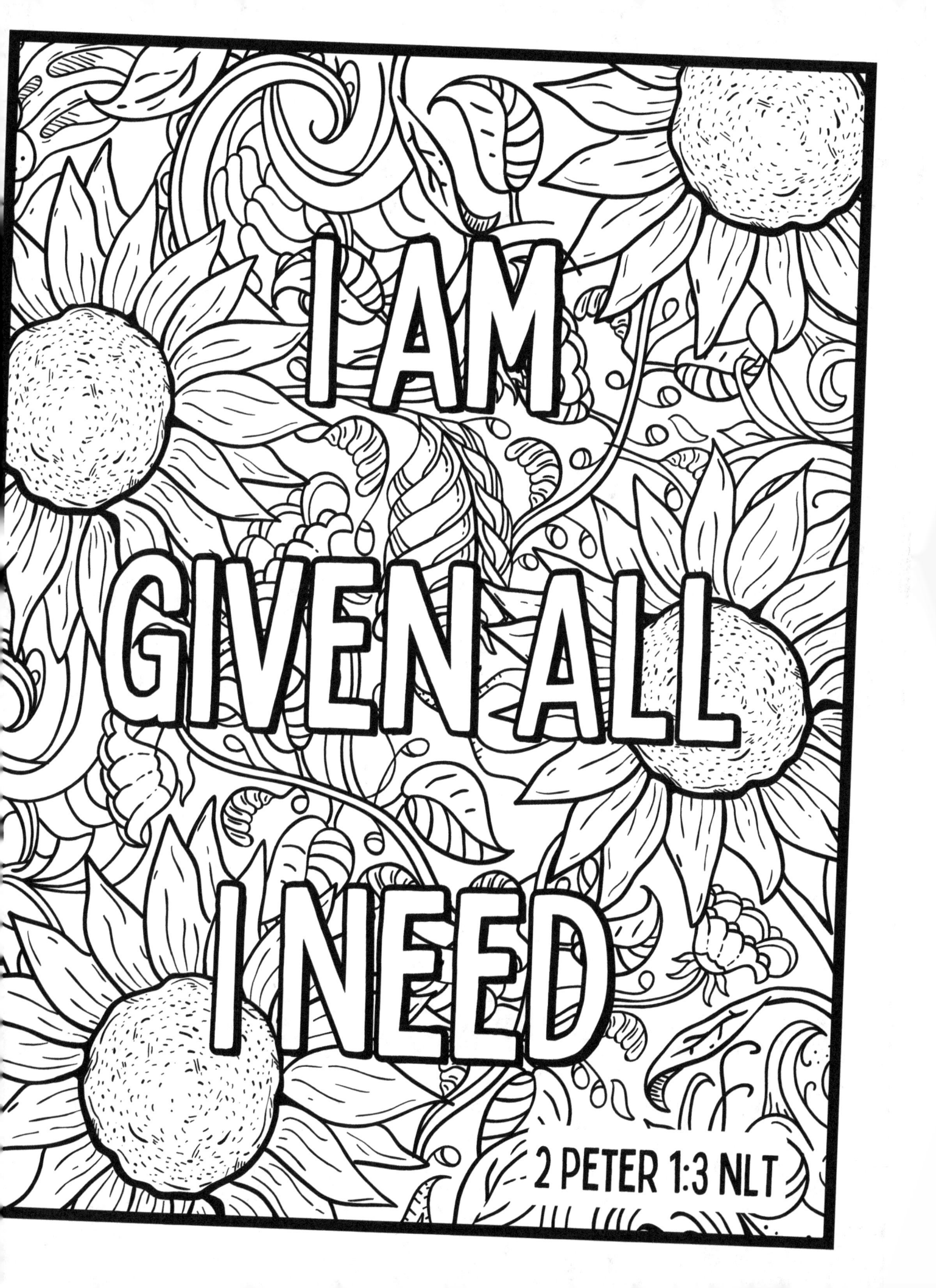

I AM

GIVEN ALL

I NEED

2 PETER 1:3 NLT

I am Given All I Need

By his divine power, God has given us everything we need for living a godly life. We have received all of this by coming to know him, the one who called us to himself by means of his marvelous glory and excellence.

2 Peter 1:3 NLT

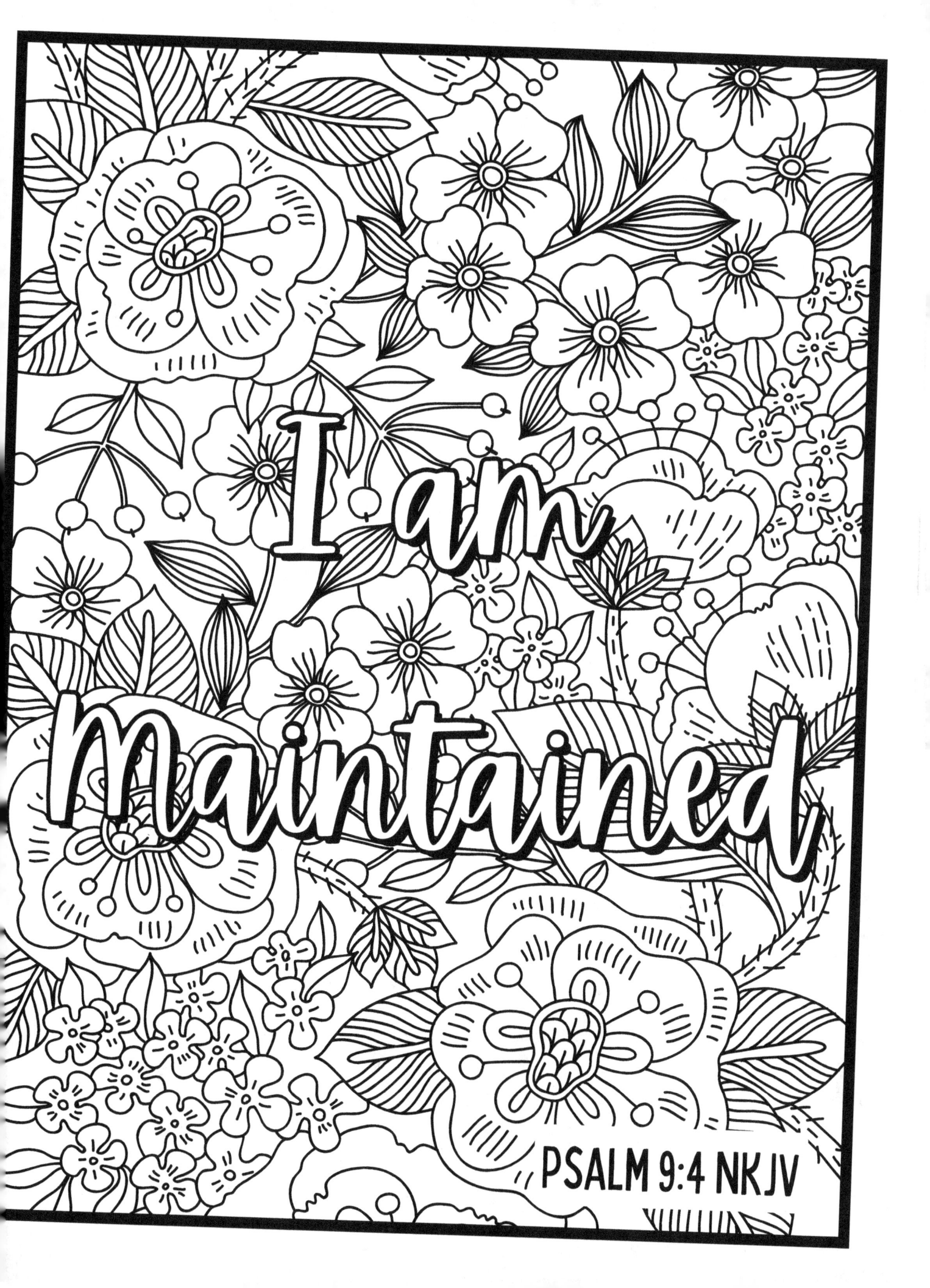

I am Maintained

PSALM 9:4 NKJV

I am Maintained

For You have maintained my right and my cause; You sat on the throne judging in righteousness.
Psalm 9:4 NKJV

I AM
SLEEPING
SOUNDLY

PROVERBS 3:24 NLT

I am Sleeping Soundly

You can go to bed without fear;
you will lie down and
sleep soundly.
Proverbs 3:24 NLT

I am a Treasured Possession

EXODUS 19:4 NIV

I am a Treasured Possession

Now if you obey me fully and keep my covenant, then out of all nations you will be my treasured possession. Although the whole earth is mine.

Exodus 19:5 NIV

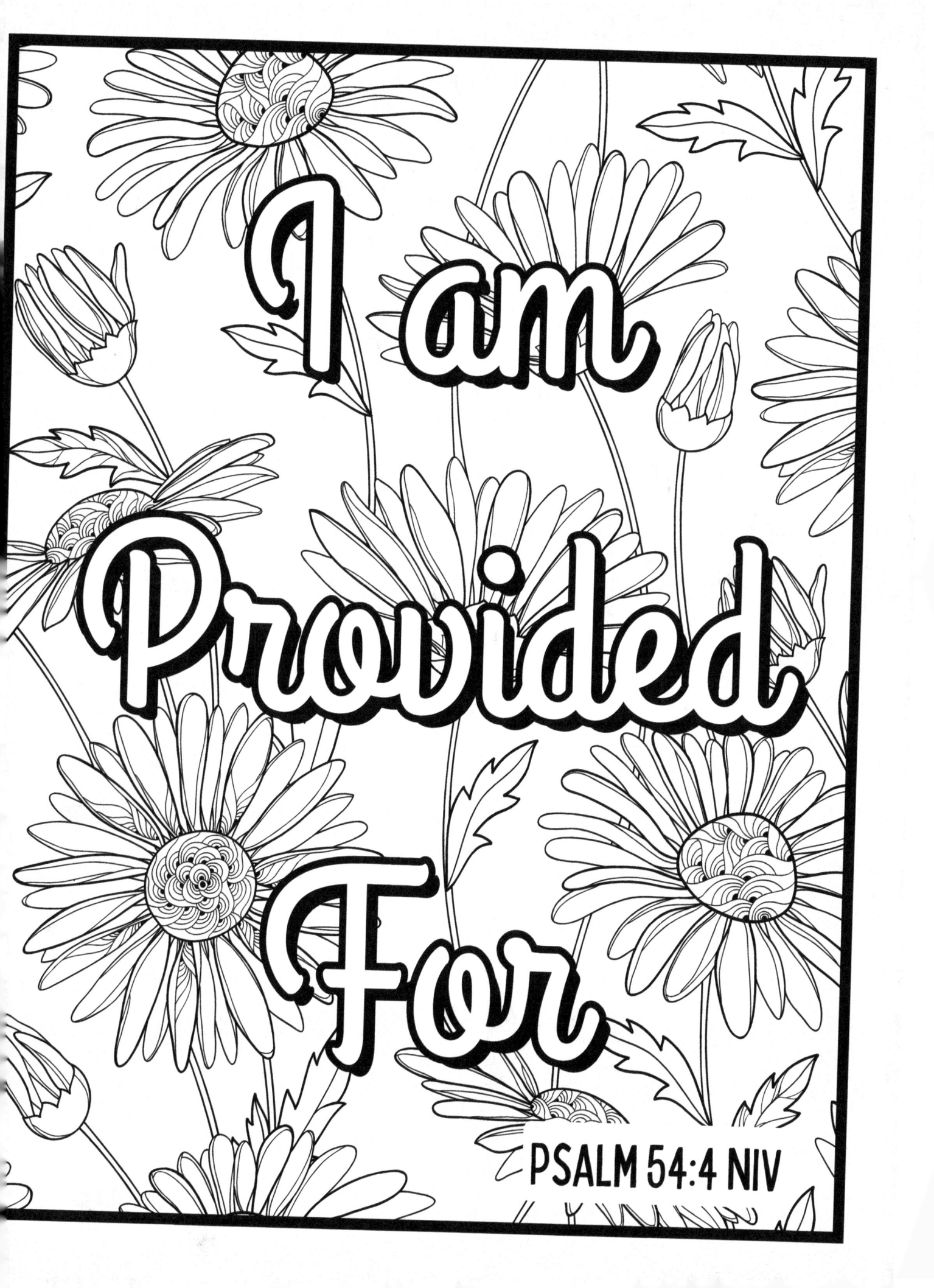

I am Provided For

PSALM 54:4 NIV

I am Provided For

Surely God is my help; the Lord is
the one who sustains me.
Psalm 54:4 NIV

I am

Cherished

JOHN 16:27 NLT

I am Cherished

. . . for the Father himself loves you dearly because you love me and believe that I came from God.
John 16:27 NLT

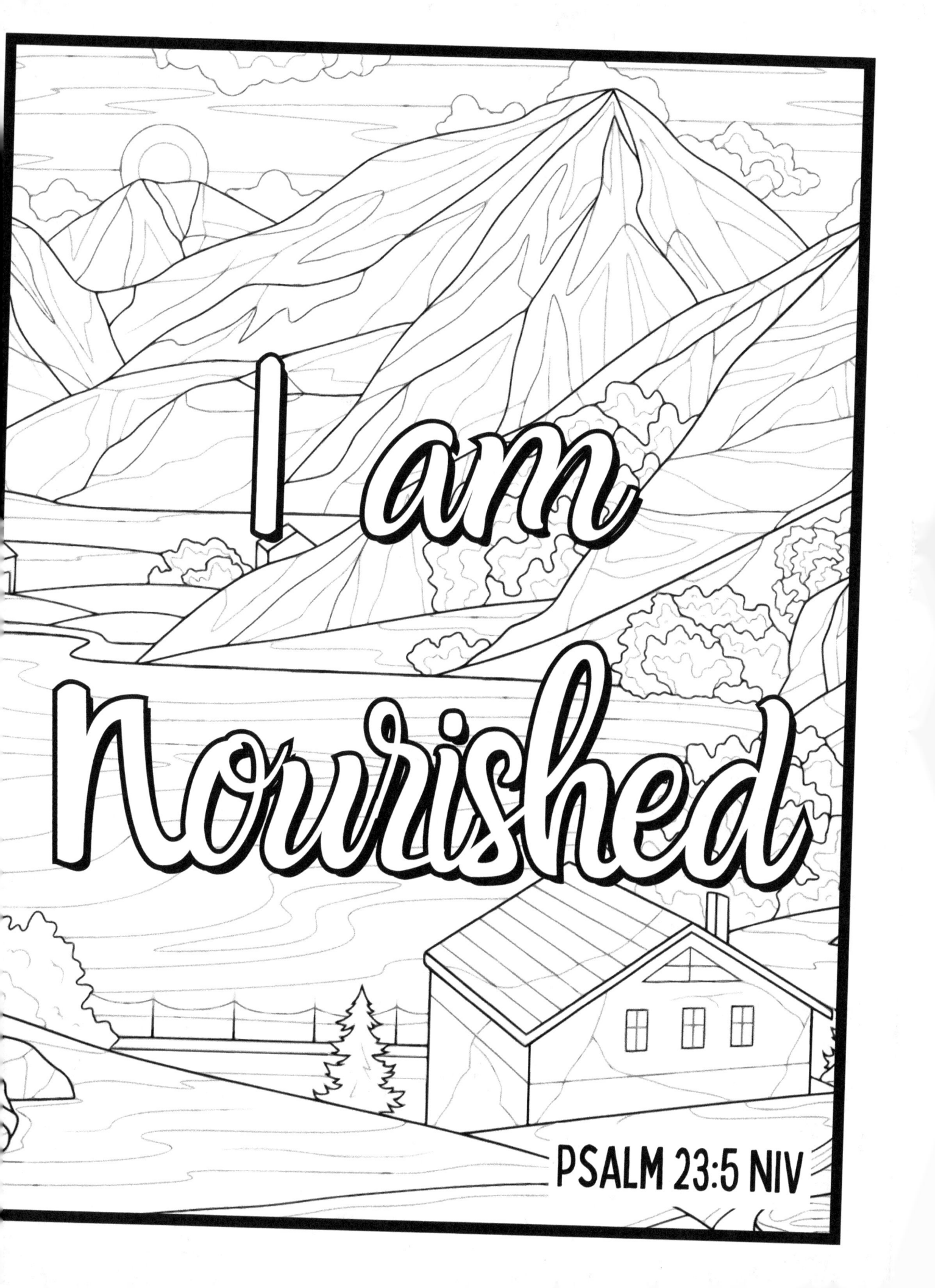

I am
Nourished

PSALM 23:5 NIV

I am Nourished

You prepare a table before me in
the presence of my enemies. You
anoint my head with oil;
my cup overflows.
Psalm 23:5 NIV

I am Restored

PSALM 23:3 NIV

I am Restored

He restores my soul. He leads
me in the paths of righteousness,
for His name's sake.
Psalm 23:3 NIV

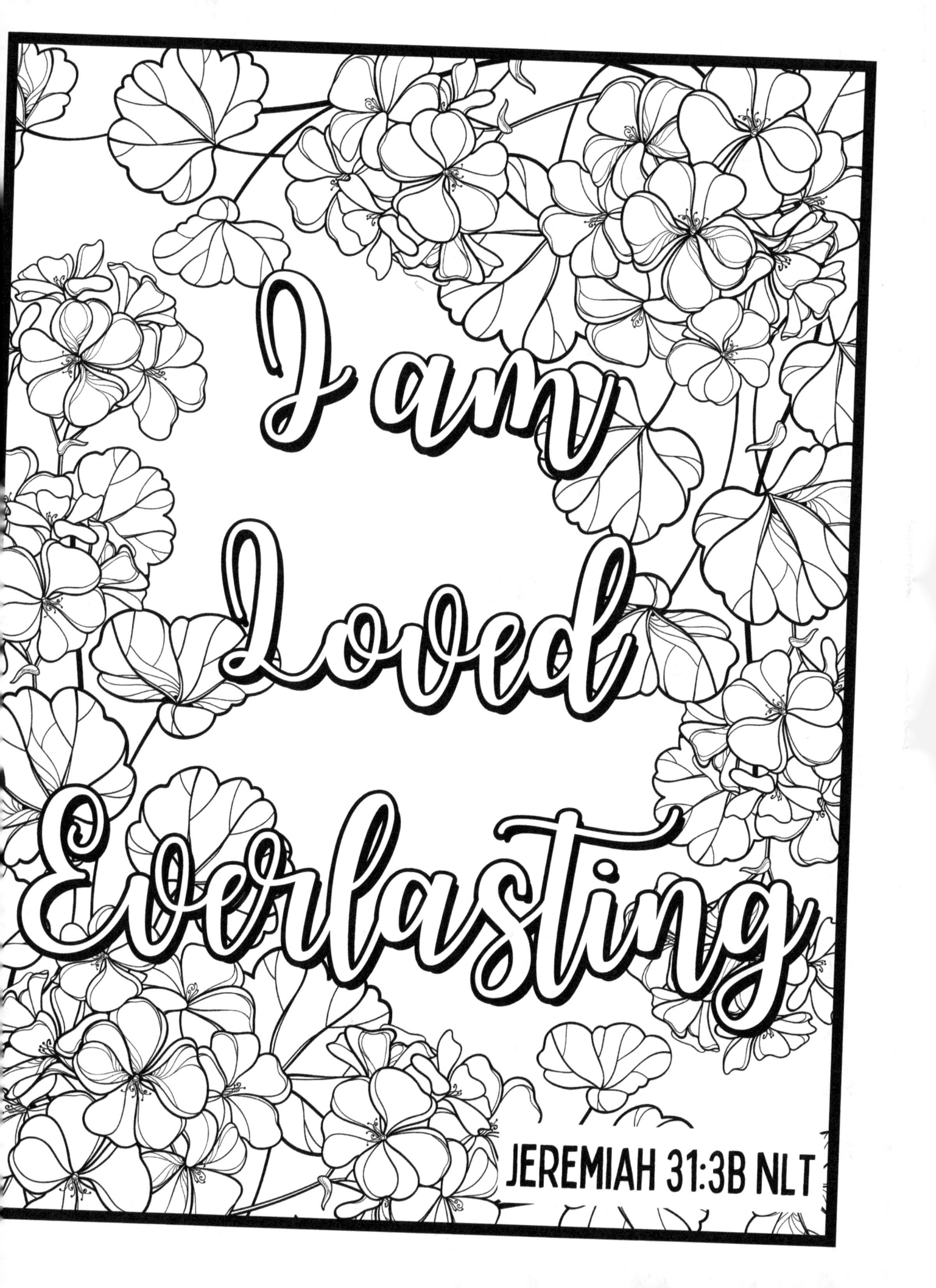

I am
Loved
Everlasting

JEREMIAH 31:3B NLT

I am Loved Everlasting

I have loved you, my people, with an everlasting love. With unfailing love I have drawn you to myself.
Jeremiah 31:3b NLT

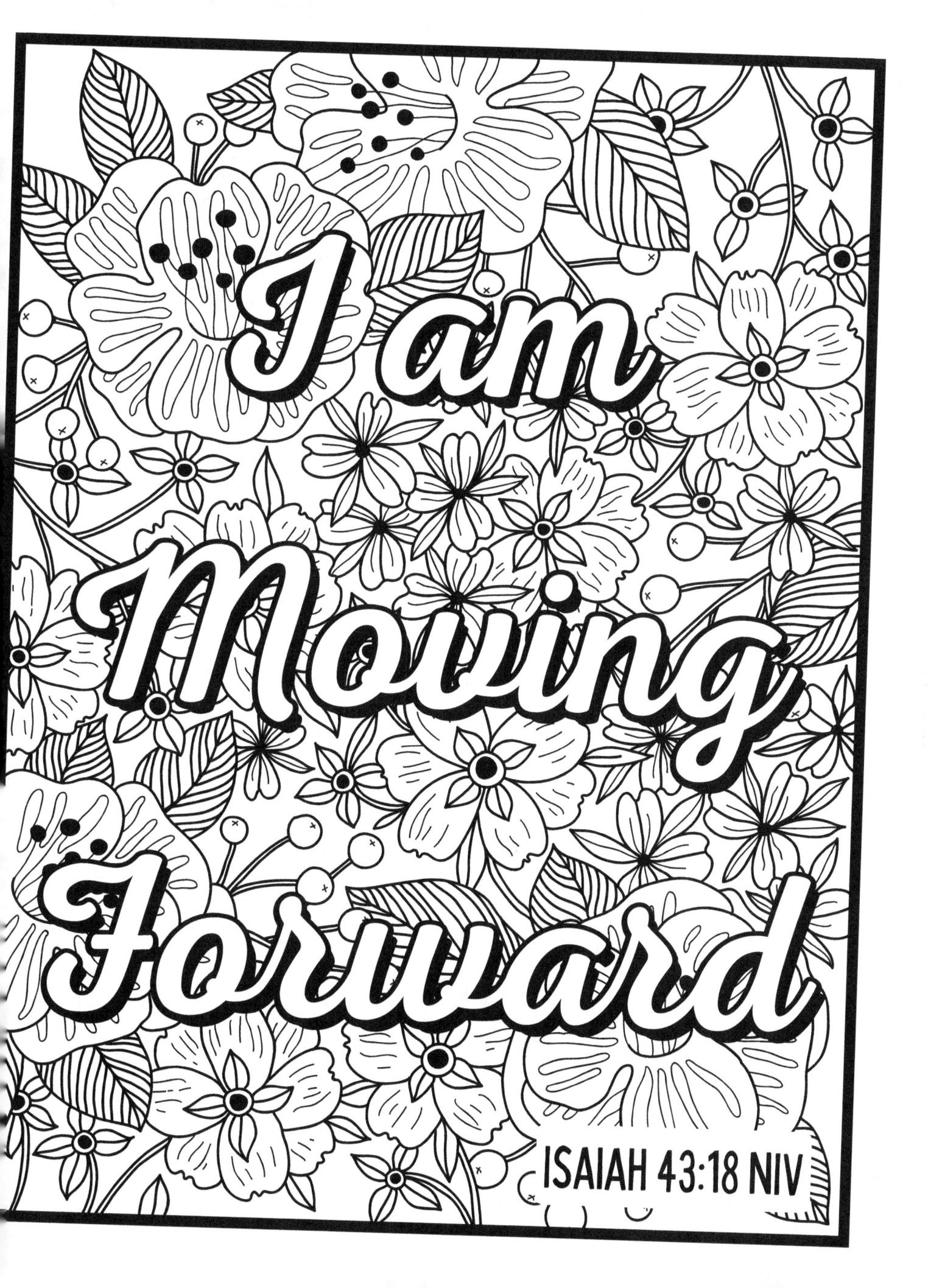

I am

Moving

Forward

ISAIAH 43:18 NIV

I am Moving Forward

Forget the former things; do
not dwell on the past.
Isaiah 43:18 NIV

I am Fearfully and Wonderfully Made

PSALM 139:14 NKJV

I am Fearfully and Wonderfully Made

I will praise You, for I am fearfully and wonderfully made; marvelous are Your works, and that my soul knows very well.

Psalm 139:14 NKJV

I am a Bearer of good fruit

COLOSSIANS 1:10 ESV

I am a Bearer of Good Fruit

So as to walk in a manner worthy of the Lord, fully pleasing to him, bearing fruit in every good work and increasing in the knowledge of God.

Colossians 1:10 ESV

I AM KEEPING

MY MIND

STEADFAST

ISAIAH 26:3 NIV

I am Keeping My Mind Steadfast

You will keep in perfect peace those whose minds are steadfast, because they trust in you.

Isaiah 26:3 NIV

The Tree of Love, LLC
Sharing Who God Says You Are

- **I am Finding Rest** - I have loved you, my people, with an everlasting love. With unfailing love I have drawn you to myself. Jeremiah 31:3b NLT

- **I am in Perfect Peace** - You will keep in perfect peace those whose minds are steadfast, because they trust in you. Trust in the Lord forever, for the Lord, the Lord himself, is the Rock eternal. Isaiah 26:3-4 NIV

- **I am Held** - Fear not, for I am with you; be not dismayed, for I am your God. I will strengthen you, yes, I will help you, I will uphold you with My righteous right hand. Isaiah 41:10 NKJV

- **I am Not Stressing** - As pressure and stress bear down on me, I find joy in your commands. Psalm 119:143 NLT

- **I am Peaceful** - I am leaving you with a gift—peace of mind and heart. And the peace I give is a gift the world cannot give. So don't be troubled or afraid. John 14:27 NLT

- **I am Helped** - For I, the Lord your God, will hold your right hand, Saying to you, 'Fear not, I will help you.' Isaiah 41:13 NKJV

- **I am Quieted by His Love** - The Lord your God in your midst, The Mighty One, will save; He will rejoice over you with gladness, He will quiet you with His love, He will rejoice over you with singing. Zephaniah 3:17 NKJV

- **I am Safe** - In peace I will lie down and sleep, for you alone, O Lord, will keep me safe. Psalm 4:8 NLT

- **I am Not Troubled** - Let not your heart be troubled; you believe in God, believe also in Me. John 14:1 NKJV

- **I am Loved Unconditionally** - Because of the Lord's great love we are not consumed, for his compassions never fail. They are new every morning; great is your faithfulness. I say to myself, "The Lord is my portion; therefore I will wait for him." Lamentations 3:22-24 NIV

- **I am Resting in the Shadows of the Almighty** - Whoever dwells in the shelter of the Most High will rest in the shadow of the Almighty. Psalm 91:1 NIV

- **I am Not Worried** - Therefore I say to you, do not worry about your life, what you will eat or what you will drink; nor about your body, what you will put on. Is not life more than food and the body more than clothing? Matthew 6:25 NKJV

- **I am Honored** - Since you were precious in My sight, You have been honored, and I have loved you; therefore I will give men for you, and people for your life. Isaiah 43:4 NKJV

- **I am Supported** - I cried out, "I am slipping!" but your unfailing love, O Lord, supported me. Psalm 94:18 NLT

- **I am Established** - For God knew his people in advance, and he chose them to become like his Son, so that his Son would be the firstborn among many brothers and sisters. Romans 8:29 NLT

- **I am Sustained** - Even to your old age and gray hairs I am he, I am he who will sustain you. I have made you and I will carry you; I will sustain you and I will rescue you. Isaiah 46:4 NIV

- **I am Consoled** - When anxiety was great within me, your consolation brought me joy. Psalm 94:19 NIV

- **I am Given All I Need** - By his divine power, God has given us everything we need for living a godly life. We have received all of this by coming to know him, the one who called us to himself by means of his marvelous glory and excellence. 2 Peter 1:3 NLT

- **I am Maintained** - For You have maintained my right and my cause; You sat on the throne judging in righteousness. Psalm 9:4 NKJV

- **I am Sleeping Soundly** - You can go to bed without fear; you will lie down and sleep soundly. Proverbs 3:24 NLT

The Tree of Love, LLC
Sharing Who God Says You Are

- **I am a Treasured Possession** - Now if you obey me fully and keep my covenant, then out of all nations you will be my treasured possession. Although the whole earth is mine. Exodus 19:5 NIV

- **I am Provided For** - Surely God is my help; the Lord is the one who sustains me. Psalm 54:4 NIV

- **I am Cherished** - . . . for the Father himself loves you dearly because you love me and believe that I came from God. John 16:27 NLT

- **I am Nourished** - You prepare a table before me in the presence of my enemies. You anoint my head with oil; my cup overflows. Psalm 23:5 NIV

- **I am Restored** - He restores my soul. He leads me in the paths of righteousness, for His name's sake. Psalm 23:3 NIV

- **I am Loved Everlasting** - I have loved you, my people, with an everlasting love. With unfailing love I have drawn you to myself. Jeremiah 31:3b NLT

- **I am Moving Forward** - Forget the former things; do not dwell on the past. Isaiah 43:18 NIV

- **I am Fearfully and Wonderfully Made** - I will praise You, for I am fearfully and wonderfully made; marvelous are Your works, and that my soul knows very well. Psalm 139:14 NKJV

- **I am a Bearer of Good Fruit** - So as to walk in a manner worthy of the Lord, fully pleasing to him, bearing fruit in every good work and increasing in the knowledge of God. Colossians 1:10 ESV

- **I am Keeping My Mind Steadfast** - You will keep in perfect peace those whose minds are steadfast, because they trust in you. Isaiah 26:3 NIV

Thank you for your purchase! If you are happy with your coloring book, please take a minute and leave us a review on Amazon.

We would love to connect with you via social media:

@TheTreeOfLoveStore

@thetreeof.love

@WhoGodSaysIAm

@thetreeoflove

https://bit.ly/TheTreeofLove-YouTube

The Tree of Love, LLC
Sharing Who God Says You Are

Check Out Our Other Coloring Books

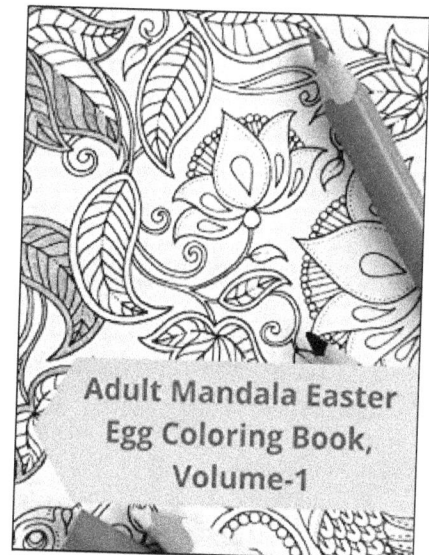

I Am Who God Says I Am!
Adult Coloring Book
20 "I Am" Statements on Floral Backgrounds with Scripture
Volume-1

I Am Who God Says I Am
Adult Coloring Book
20 "I Am" Statements on Floral Backgrounds with Scripture
Volume-2

I am Loved Everlasting
20 Floral Coloring Pages With God's Truth of His Everlasting Love For You

Inspiring Bible Verses on Floral Backgrounds Coloring Book for Adults

Encouraging Bible Verses Coloring Book
20 Floral Designs With God's Word

Adult Mandala Easter Egg Coloring Book, Volume-1

The Tree of Love, LLC
Sharing Who God Says You Are

THE TREE OF LOVE'S MISSION
To put a shirt on 1-million people
"Sociologists tell us that even the most introverted person will influence 10,000 people in his or her lifetime." ~ John Maxwell

1 T-Shirt = 10,000 Influenced
For every t-shirt purchased, The Tree of Love LLC, will donate $1 to *The Gideons International,*
www.Gideons.org

Shop Our Online Store: https://thetreeoflove.org/

The Tree of Love™

Who God Says I Am

God Loves Me

thetreeoflove.org

www.ingramcontent.com/pod-product-compliance
Lightning Source LLC
Chambersburg PA
CBHW080947050426
42337CB00055B/4659